Lord Sell A Cow

Lord Sell A Cow

Jenny Desmet

The Pentland Press Limited
Edinburgh • Cambridge • Durham • USA

First published in 1999 by
The Pentland Press Ltd.
1 Hutton Close
South Church
Bishop Auckland
Durham

British Library Cataloguing in Publication Data.
A Catalogue record for this book is available
from the British Library.

ISBN 1 85821 709 1

Typeset by CBS, Martlesham Heath, Ipswich, Suffolk
Printed and bound by Antony Rowe Ltd., Chippenham

I wish to dedicate this book to Christians everywhere, encouraging them to step out in faith and prove God in their own lives.

Remembering God is no respecter of persons. His promises are not for a chosen few, but we may all claim our inheritance.

I also wish to dedicate this book to the memory of my late mother Mrs Marjorie Gritt. She was a wonderful Christian lady who touched the lives of many people, her faith has been my inspiration. And to my wonderful husband Marcel for his faith, love and commitment to the call of God on our lives.

Contents

Foreword

I count it a privilege and an honour to write the foreword to this very precious book.

I have known Jenny for many years, and listened to the story of her life with great interest. Often I've thought how wonderful it would be if she wrote a book all about it, to bless and encourage others as much as it has blessed me. So you can imagine how thrilled I was to hear that she had done just that. I know you will find it difficult to put the book down once you start reading it, and like me, you will say, I wish there were more.

Jenny was very privileged to have a very godly Mother, and it meant so much to her. I'm sure her Mother often prayed that Jenny would grow up to serve the Lord, and her prayers were answered.

As you read this book 'Lord Sell A Cow' you will see God's hand was upon her from a very early age. Her faith for the Lord grew as did her love for all she met. Her one desire was that everyone that she met would love Jesus as she did.

Jenny, like all young ladies wanted a boyfriend, and the way it came about was just wonderfully exciting. The Lord chose her boy friend for her. This story will thrill young ladies wanting to make the right choice, and older folk will just want to praise the Lord. As soon as Jenny saw Marcel she knew he was the Lord's choice for her, and they have now had many happy years together serving the Lord, and the marriage was truly made in heaven.

The way ahead was not always easy, there were many times of great testing, but they never lost their faith, and God honoured them for it. To know the wonderful answers to prayer, you will need to read the book.

I've read many Christian books, but this one is different, and it really gripped me.

Like the Apostle Paul, Jenny and Marcel know the secret of being content with plenty or nothing. To be in their company is something really special and as you leave them you feel you have been with Jesus. They have a wonderful gift of being able to come alongside folk, they have a listening ear, and you feel the Lord is just speaking through them.

Their apprenticeship with the Lord has been an experience that has taught them to use every difficulty as a stepping stone to get closer to the Lord, and what He has done for them He can do for all who ask Him.

I pray that this book will bring Hope, Faith and Comfort to all who read it.

Francis W. Jeffries

Preface

I count it a great joy and privilege to read this first book of my dear wife Jenny. Not only was I blessed very much, but it was also an opportunity to reminisce on God's goodness to us during our 32 years of marriage.

It is good to look back and see how God's plans and purposes have unfolded. Not only on the mountain top experiences, but also as we travelled through the valleys. God has continually shown us His faithfulness as He brought us through many varying situations.

The Christian road is not always an easy road, but God is always there, even in our darkest moments. It is in such times that we experience the preciousness of the true and living God.

My prayer is that this book will be a great blessing to all who read it and that they will be encouraged to reach out and find God in a deeper way.

Revd Marcel Jules Desmet.

Chapter 1

Lord Sell a Cow

I was just eight years old when I had my first real encounter with God. It took place in the Guild Hall in Southampton one Sunday evening during an after-church rally. I was sitting about eight rows from the front, in an end of row seat next to the fire exit doors. Sitting with me were my Mum, sister and some folk from our church. This special meeting was the last night of a campaign led by evangelist Lorne Fox. In fact it was his last ever meeting, as he was killed in a plane crash the following day.

I was brought up in a Christian home. My Mum was very special; although we never had much in the way of money or worldly possessions, we had just so much love. There was enough love for us and all the children in the village. Mum became a second Mum to almost everyone she met. She always had time to listen and would get really enthusiastic about any topic we wanted to discuss. If a friend came home with us, they were always made welcome. Mum used to say, 'If you can't bring your friends home, then maybe you shouldn't be going out with them.'

Sunday school anniversary was a big day for us; we would practise our pieces for weeks before the actual day. Then the day before, Mum would draw the water from the well, fill up the big boiler in the yard and light a fire under it so there would be plenty of hot water for our baths and hair washes. You see, we didn't have a bathroom or drains, so it was a big task for Mum to bath us four children. She would drag the big galvanized bath into the lounge (it wasn't really a lounge, it was the only room we had in our four-roomed bungalow that wasn't a bedroom.) She usually bathed my sister and I first, then added some more water for the boys before dragging the bath into her bedroom and adding more hot water for herself and Dad to bath. Afterwards she would take the water out a bucketful at a time and pour it onto the garden since we didn't have drains.

The night before Sunday School anniversary she would also bath a couple of our friends (who came from a different kind of home than ours) and do all our hair in rag curlers, so we would all look nice for our special day. I could tell you lots about that very special lady whom God allowed me to have as my Mum.

Dad was away a lot working as a long distance lorry driver and spent most Sundays preaching on the local Methodist circuit. I have two older brothers and an older sister, which makes me the baby of the family. This fact I was often reminded of, for right up until my Mum's death she always introduced me as her baby! Even when I was head and shoulders taller than she was.

Up until the age of eight I used to go to church three times each Sunday. On Sunday morning I would go to the Pentecostal church, then Sunday school in the afternoon, and in the evening I would go to the Pentecostal church one week and the Methodist church with Gran the following week. Gran was another special lady.

I really loved going to church and always dreamed of becoming a missionary when I grew up. I can remember as a very young child I used to help Dad take the services when he went preaching. I would lead the service and give the bible reading. In some churches I had to stand on a chair to see over the pulpit, but I realise now what a good training ground it was.

We didn't have a television, in fact we didn't even have electricity. Our evenings were spent singing around the piano by Tilley lamp or candlelight if we had run out of paraffin. Sometimes we listened to Biggles or Larry the Lamb on a very crackly radio, when we had the money to have the accumulator charged. During the long hot summer days we spent much of our time on the common near our home. Mum would pack us up a bag of jam sandwiches and we would go for a picnic, always leaving straight after dinner. We usually arrived home around two o'clock after eating our picnic! None of us had a watch so we had no idea of time.

We all had a wonderful childhood, and Mum had such a simple, uncomplicated childlike faith. We often saw the hand of the Lord supplying our needs in miraculous ways. When there was a need Mum would say, 'Lord, you own the cattle on a thousand hills, please sell another cow.'

Mum was very faithful in her giving to the Lord. Often she would give money that she couldn't really afford to give and one day I can remember her coming home from a meeting and bursting into tears as she saw a box of vegetables on the doorstep. We had a bowl of vegetable soup for our meal, I guess God sent an angel to deliver it in time for tea.

Another time I remember was when Mum needed new shoes, the soles of her shoes had long since worn through. Each day she would take a piece of cardboard from a cornflake box and cut out new soles to place in her shoes. She prayed and asked God for some shoes. That same afternoon as she was walking to her Women's meeting, her sister called out that she had received a parcel with two pairs of shoes in and they didn't fit her. Mum immediately replied, 'They will fit me.' Aunty Jess said she was just being stupid, how could she possibly know they would fit her, she hadn't even seen them.

Mum called back 'God knows my size.' Guess who had two pairs of shoes that were a perfect fit? Now that is the kind of faith I was brought up on.

I gave my life to the Lord every time there was an appeal, just to get another free St John's gospel. I didn't want them for myself, I used to give them to other children.

That night in the Guild Hall in Southampton I knew for the first time that God had placed His call on my life. During the service there was a little boy sitting on a pair of steps on the stage behind one of the big red curtains, I could see him from where I was sitting. He could see everything from there, people going forward to receive Christ into their lives, others going forward for healing. From where I was sitting I could only hear what was happening. So I prayed 'Please God, make my Dad an evangelist so I can sit on the stage and see what is happening.'

It was then that the Lord spoke to me. He told me that one day I would be an evangelist and do all the things that this man was doing. I was so excited and every time I recall those words I have that same sense of excitement. It was wonderful knowing the call of God on my life.

Chapter 2

Childhood Memories

I can recall the first time I was allowed to go to Sunday school with my brothers and sister, I was just two years old. It was in the Methodist church a short distance from our home. I remember being lifted up onto a dark brown pew. My feet were nowhere near the floor, I was petrified. I loved singing, because then I was lifted off that horrible pew and my feet were firmly on the ground.

We all enjoyed singing in our house. Mum even had an old treadle sewing machine and that was a 'Singer'. Most evenings would find us all singing hymns and choruses around the piano. My favourite one was 'It isn't any trouble just to S.M.I.L.E. Smile away your troubles, they will vanish like a bubble, if you only take the trouble just to S.M.I.L.E.'

Our dog Perky used to join in the singing. He would howl in time with the music. I remember one day a neighbour came rushing in shouting 'Quick, quick, Perky must have been hit by a car, he's making terrible noises and he's lying in the ditch.' Mum went running up the road, only to find Perky 'singing' in the ditch. Mum had a very special, gentle voice and she blessed many people over the years with her anointed singing. Dad's voice was quite different, he had singing lessons until he was almost 80 years old. His voice was very loud and powerful (ask the neighbours!).

I don't know if your home was like this, but I am sure if I went indoors with my eyes closed I could tell what day of the week it was by the smell. Saturday was the smell of a roast dinner. We always had roast on Saturday because Sunday was a very busy day for us all. Sunday was the smell of 'Bubble and Squeak'. Mum always cooked enough on Saturday to fry up on Sunday for a quick lunch. Monday was the damp smell of the washing, especially when it had to be dried indoors around the open fire.

I really loved the Friday smell, because that was the day when Mum polished the furniture and the lino. When we got home from school Mum would spread polish on the floor in the passage, and we would tie rags onto our feet and slide up and down the length of the passage polishing the floor until it really shone.

Mum had a very best friend whom we called Auntie Rene. One day when they obviously wanted a bit of peace and quiet, I was sent down to the bottom of the garden to sing to the chickens. I was told if I sang nicely they would lay an egg for my tea. Sure enough, the chickens always laid me a brown egg which I would carry home carefully and have for my tea.

Actually those chickens played quite a role in my early years. We were told in Sunday school that we should tell our friends about Jesus if we wanted them to go to heaven. I certainly wanted the chickens to go to heaven so I used to tell them about Jesus and sing to them every afternoon. This special friendship carried on until I went to school.

At school I can remember making children learn bible verses if they wanted to be my friend. So I can see God's hand on my life from a very young age.

Chapter 3

I Wanted More

I had a very loving, uncomplicated childhood, and soon became an active person in the churches I attended. I taught in the Pentecostal Sunday school and took part in the Methodist Christian Endeavour, where I took a very active part in the discussions we had each week. I think poor Mr King wished I wasn't there. You see the Methodist Church didn't accept the baptism in the Holy Spirit and the Pentecostal Church did, so I used to take every available opportunity to try to show them 'the truth'. It really was amazing just how I managed to turn every weekly topic discussion into the need to receive the baptism of the Holy Spirit. The strange thing was at that time I hadn't even received it myself. This wonderful experience became a reality to me at a Youth camp several years later.

At the age of fifteen I left school and two days later I started my first job. This gave me a tremendous sense of freedom, I could now afford to go into Southampton and attend a real live church. I just wanted more than the village churches could offer me. They just talked about the wonderful things God had done in the past, but nothing seemed to be happening now.

I joined the Elim church at Park Road and soon became a choir member and joined the youth group and prayer group. I really enjoyed it for a time. Then one Easter Monday I went with the church to the Royal Albert Hall in London and as we were all singing 'Lest I forget Gethsemane' I felt such a powerful anointing of the Holy Spirit. It was wonderful, and the feeling stayed with me for days afterwards. So I went to the minister and asked him why we never had that anointing on the meetings at our church, only to be told that sort of thing was only for special rallies, not for everyday services.

I remember one Sunday evening I gave my first message in tongues. It came as a total surprise to me. Mrs Tyre was sitting next to me in the choir, and she gently placed her hand on my knee and whispered, 'Don't worry dear, that was a message in tongues.' My father immediately got up and started praying. I knew that wasn't the interpretation, and he seemed to go on for ever, I was just willing him to stop so I could hear the interpretation. He did eventually stop, then to my surprise the elder who was taking the service because the pastor was away, got up and rebuked me from the pulpit for daring to give a tongue when there was no interpreter present. I didn't understand, but was later told that only the pastor had the gift of interpretation. I felt very hurt and sad that I would never know what God wanted to say through the tongue I gave. However this experience gave me a real hunger for more of God.

I soon became dissatisfied with the youth meeting, it seemed unless you were part of the 'clique' you were never asked to take part in any of the meetings. All the time I still had a burning desire to work for God.

Each Sunday evening four of us used to go out onto Shirley High Street inviting people to come to the service. Jim Woolgar used to lead our little group. He was a converted alcoholic, I remember when he got saved and immediately he had such a gentle, loving spirit, and whenever I saw him he always seemed to be telling someone about the Lord. I learned a lot from Jim, and really thank the Lord for the privilege of ever knowing him.

I approached the Pastor about the possibility of going to Bible College. His reply was, 'You could never afford that' and he seemed to laugh at the idea of me even wanting to go. I was getting more and more dissatisfied with the church, especially the youth meeting. Nobody seemed to want bible studies, each week they used to have programmes that I found childish.

When I got off the bus one Wednesday night, instead of turning left into Park Road I started turning right and going into the youth meeting at the Assemblies of God church in Millbrook Road. This meeting was much deeper spiritually, at least they used to have bible studies each week, but still something was missing. I wanted more. It was then that I was invited to the Co-op rooms at the bus station, to a meeting. This was really different.

Although there were only a handful of people present, they really seemed to believe what they were preaching, and from the first meeting I felt again the anointing that I had experienced in the Albert Hall. Mind you, they did some very funny things, like all praying in tongues together, dancing and banging tambourines. It was strange, but something used to draw me to those meetings. I immediately felt a love there that was missing from the other churches I had been to.

Things began to happen, people got saved, healed and baptized in the Holy Spirit. We had an all night prayer meeting every month and after each meeting there was always a special anointing on the weekend services. Each Saturday evening we used to have an open-air service outside Dunn's hat shop where we had a ready-made congregation as people would be queuing to get into the two cinemas.

We would then have a meeting in the Co-op rooms. Sundays we had a morning service, then we would go down to Speakers' Corner in Southsea for an open air meeting before returning to Southampton for another open-air meeting before the evening service. We had outreaches or meetings most evenings of the week. It was great, I really loved it. I learned much from the time I spent at these services. I found a new freedom in worship and learned how to trust the Lord.

Chapter 4

The School Of Faith

Now that I had a job which paid me a set salary every month so I knew exactly how much money I had to spend or save, the Lord began to teach me to trust Him in financial matters.

Once I was at a meeting and I really felt I should give a certain sum of money to a missionary, knowing if I did, then I would not have enough money to pay my bus fares to work for that week. I really had to travel by bus because I lived in West Wellow, a small village about fourteen miles from my place of work in Portswood, Southampton. The feeling became stronger as the meeting progressed, so I said, 'Well Lord I will give this money, but I am trusting you to get me to work.' Monday morning came and I left home at the usual time (7.30 a.m.) to catch the bus, only I had an empty purse. I prayed all the way to the bus stop, reminding the Lord I needed a lift. Just before the bus was due someone I knew stopped and offered me a lift. Coming home a similar thing happened. In fact I had lifts every day that week. I must add that no one knew I had no money, not even my Mum, and we were the best of friends. Of course I testified of the Lord's provision afterwards to encourage others to be obedient to the Lord's promptings.

Secondly, I had always had a desire to visit Switzerland. Dad offered to pay for me to go with a school trip during my last year at Bartley School, but I refused because my brothers and sister had never had this opportunity and it didn't seem fair that I should be spoilt in this way. I determined as soon as I could afford to pay for myself I would go there for a holiday.

After finishing college I began to save for the trip. I then saw an advertisement in a church magazine for a youth holiday in Switzerland.

I immediately booked. Being on a set salary I knew how much I could afford. After taking out my tithes, offerings and usual living expenses, I knew I had only £5 extra cash. This wasn't a problem because at last my dream of a trip to Switzerland was about to become a reality. I was so excited. But then something happened which I had not expected.

A friend invited me to a youth meeting at Romsey Elim church, where a preacher was speaking about the need for a group of young people to give up their summer holidays and go to Belgium and work in evangelistic outreach teams. This sounded great, something I would love to do, but I knew I couldn't afford it.

All through the meeting I was having a battle with God. I knew He wanted me to go and I knew I couldn't afford it. The time was no problem, because I had school holidays, but the money was. As the meeting progressed I was thinking that it really wasn't fair if God expected me to give up this dream holiday in Switzerland which I had been planning in my mind for the last four years. At the end of the meeting the preacher said, 'All I need from you tonight is a £5 deposit and for you to send the rest four weeks before we go.' Before I could stop myself I was out the front paying my last £5 as a deposit.

I went home feeling happy knowing I was doing the right thing, but a bit cross with God because I felt sure I would have to cancel my trip to Switzerland. On Monday morning I went into work only to find the head teacher in quite a panic.

'What have you done?' she asked.

'Nothing,' I replied.

'Well you must have done something really bad. The chief education officer has just phoned and she wants you to go immediately to the civic centre to see her.'

I hadn't a clue why she would send for me, and of course I was imagining the worst on that bus trip into Southampton centre. What if she sacks me. How am I going to pay for this trip to Belgium? Of course I had a little moan at God, He was the one who told me to book for this evangelistic outreach team. Where would I get another job in the middle of term? Who would have me if I had been sacked? Why should I be sacked, I hadn't done anything wrong? I loved working with the children at the diagnostic unit, why should I have to leave? I was getting in quite a spin.

I soon found myself walking down the long corridors of the civic centre, through endless fire doors until I at last came to the chief education officer's office. I knocked on the door. She didn't call out, 'Come in' as I expected, but she came to the door, smiling. I felt sure this was the softly, softly approach and any minute this very pleasant attitude would change. But it didn't. She talked to me about my job, saying how pleased everyone was with my work. After what seemed an age, she said, 'I'm afraid I have an apology to make to you.'

I thought, 'This is it, she is going to break it to me gently.' But she didn't.

To my surprise she said, 'I'm afraid wc have been paying you on the wrong salary scale, we should have paid you more. Now you can of course demand to have the back pay immediately, but if you wouldn't mind, it would be easier for us to pay you the monies owing on your next pay cheque.'

Mind! me mind! of course I didn't mind. I left that office on cloud nine, praising the Lord for His wonderful provision. By the way, I had enough to pay for the trip to Belgium, buy a camera and still had spending money. Isn't the Lord good?

The school of faith isn't always easy, but it is wonderful to be able to look back and see just what God has done.

Chapter 5

Lord I Want A Boyfriend

Here I was nearly twenty-one years old, and the only person in my family who wasn't married. I had lots of friends who were boys, but I felt it was time to think seriously about marriage. At this rate I would soon be an old maid! So I did what all Christians should do, I asked the Lord for the partner of His choice.

As I lay in bed praying this prayer one night, I felt God was saying, 'Seek ye first the kingdom of God and His righteousness and all these things shall be added unto you.'

'OK God,' I said, 'I won't ever pray this prayer again, but I will seek to do your will and entrust my future into your hands.'

I felt at peace. The next big thing in my life was the planned trip to Belgium then the trip to Switzerland, so I had plenty to occupy my mind. My trip to Belgium was a real missionary experience.

There were fourteen of us on the team and we slept in sleeping bags on the bare floor boards. (Well some did, but I took a lilo to sleep on). It was great fun; seven, mainly teenage girls sleeping rough in the same room. If one moved we all had to move, so if anyone wanted to turn over, they would call out, 'Turn over' and we would all turn over.

Every night without fail the girl next to me would wait until I was asleep then she would pull the stopper out of my lilo pillow and my head would slowly sink to the floor. It's a very strange sensation waking up and finding your head sinking into a pillow as it deflates. This action meant that we all had to move to make space for me to pump up the pillow.

Another fun thing that I particularly remember was the time we decided to go shopping to buy gifts to take home. I wanted a musical windmill. We spent ages outside the shop flapping our arms around, deciding how we were going to ask for this windmill. When we had stopped giggling and come to the conclusion we could just point at it, we stepped inside the shop. To our utter amazement, the shop assistant said ''Ello ducks, and what can I do you for?' in the broadest cockney accent.

It wasn't all fun and games, we did some serious work too. One day another girl and myself were out distributing tracts in the houses when I slipped and twisted my ankle badly. It suddenly swelled up like a balloon and I couldn't walk on it. We decided we must pray, and as we did the swelling went down and I was able to walk normally again. Praise God.

One of the highlights of this trip was when we prayed for a Belgian man to receive the baptism of the Holy Spirit. He began to praise and worship God in English. I thought he knew English and after the service was over I tried speaking to him in English, but he didn't understand a word I was saying. This was the first time I had ever heard anyone speaking English when they were baptized with the Holy Spirit.

I was in Belgium for two weeks, spending the first week in Oostende and moving to Ghent for the second week. During the first week I really felt that God was telling me to stay in Oostende for the second week. So I approached the team leader and he said there was no way I could stay. Arrangements had been made for us to move on as a team and a new team would be coming to Oostende. I went back to the Lord and told Him I was willing to stay, but there wasn't any possibility I would be allowed to. He reminded me that when He opens a door no man can close it. So I left it with Him.

Saturday was moving day, so I packed up my belongings and they were all secured to the top of the van we were to travel in. Everyone was sitting in the van excited about the move, but I remained standing outside, waiting for the Lord to do something if He really wanted me to stay. Then it happened. One of the team members had an epileptic fit; she was not well enough to travel and would need to stay in Oostende to recover. Someone would have to stay with her. Guess who that person was?

Yes when God opens a door, even if it seems a totally impossible situation, no man can close that door.

Now why did God want me to remain in Oostende? Well I was soon to find out. In the early hours of Sunday morning the new team arrived with a pastor and his wife who were responsible for cooking the meals. They took one look at the 'first class' missionary conditions they were expected to work in and promptly walked out and went to a hotel.

Perhaps I should explain. The kitchen was in the basement, there was no electricity, only one tap with cold water and just two small gas rings to cook for twenty-one people. The only light was candle light and a little light which came through the windows which were at pavement level.

I don't think they liked the idea of sleeping on the floor or walking down three flights of stairs to the loo and sharing it with twenty-one young people. Maybe they didn't fancy washing in the backyard using the same bowl as twenty-one other people either.

Guess who ended up doing the cooking? Yes, it was me.

It was hard work and difficult planning just how to have a meal cooked on time without it getting cold or overcooked. But a lot of prayers went into every meal and we all survived. I was still able to join in some of the afternoon outreaches and the evening services. At the end of each day, around midnight we would all gather in the candlelit basement for a prayer meeting. We had some very precious times there.

On the last night God gave me a vision of the back view of myself in a wedding dress, and my husband-to-be standing by my side.

I said 'Lord, that's no good, let us turn around so I can see who he is.' We turned around and I saw Marcel standing by my side. Now Marcel was the Pastor of the church in Oostende and he was also our interpreter.

I was so excited, but I couldn't tell anybody, especially not Marcel. Well, it would be rather strange going up to a man and saying 'Oh, by the way, God has just shown me we are going to be married.'

Chapter 6

Swept Off My Feet

If anyone had told me it was possible to fall madly in love with someone and them not even know it, I would never have believed it. But it was definitely happening to me. I travelled home from Belgium leaving my heart behind me.

Marcel had asked me if I would send him an English copy of the New Testament, so I sent it a few days after returning home. Again I had to leave the rest to the Lord. At least now Marcel had my address, so if the Lord spoke to him about me he would be able to contact me.

After a couple of weeks I received a letter from Marcel thanking me for the bible and asking if I could arrange any meetings for him as he was planning to come to England on a preaching tour. Great, this gave me the excuse to write back. It was very difficult writing and not mentioning my feelings for him. I knew when it was God's perfect timing he would tell Marcel.

Our letters continued, until one day Marcel wrote a special letter telling me of his feelings for me. There were letters passing between us regularly. In fact, living in a small village has some advantages. Our village postman somehow learned that the post from Belgium was special, so if he was a little late arriving and I was already on the bus going to work, he would drive up the road and stop the bus. He would then bring me my letter shouting, 'Special delivery'. Often the conductor on the bus would ask if the post had arrived yet as I got on.

I planned to go to Belgium for the Christmas holidays and stay with some missionaries. The wife came from Southampton, Marcel lived with them. During my stay Marcel popped the magical question and we became engaged.

When I got onto the bus again on my first day back to work, my friends were shouting 'Take off your gloves, take off your gloves.' It was freezing cold, but I took them off. 'I told you' shouted Mary, 'I told you she'd be engaged.' Well really, what was the point of waiting; we both knew this was God's will. I must say here, that I did not tell Marcel about the vision until after we were married.

We decided we would get married in the summer of 1967. The only problem was finding a time when we could fit it in. I was booked to be in a Convention in London, then there was the outreach team again in Belgium, and a four-week I.G.O. (International Gospel Outreach) Convention in Southsea so the earliest date was September 2nd.

Lord you will need to sell another cow, as we have no money for a wedding.

At first I was quite happy to get married in a suit to save the expense of a wedding dress, but the Lord reminded me of the vision where I was definitely wearing a wedding dress. Where on earth would I get a wedding dress big enough? 'Lord, it's over to you again,' I prayed.

A few weeks later I came home from work and felt I should look in the 'For sale' items in the *Echo* for a wedding dress. There was actually one there in my size, the only problem was that it didn't state the price. I went upstairs and worked out my finances! It didn't take long, I only had £12 in total. Mum thought it would be a good idea to just go and see it, so my brother Dave drove me into Southampton.

When I got to the door and rang the bell, I thought to myself 'This is stupid, who is going to sell a wedding dress my size for £12?' A lady answered the door and invited us in. She was a backslider, having previously gone to the Elim church in Portsmouth. She seemed very interested in my forthcoming marriage and was pleased I was going to marry a pastor. We had a cup of tea and after what seemed an age, she said she would get the dress. It was beautiful, made from heavy white brocade material and it had a long train. There was a beautiful coronet and headdress. The moment I saw it I knew it would cost far more than £12. I kept asking, 'How much are you asking for it?' but she avoided answering. 'Try it on,' she kept saying. 'But I doubt if I can afford it,' I said.

'Well,' she said, 'I paid a lot for the material, there is twenty yards in it, then I had it made,' but she wouldn't give me any indication how much she wanted. All she would say was, 'Try it on.' So I did. It fitted like a glove, (well, God knew my size). My brother even said how nice it looked. 'You will have the veil and coronet as well won't you?' 'But how much are you asking for it?' I asked again. She thought for a moment 'You can have it all for . . . £12.' I was totally delighted. Thank you Lord. I spoke to her about her need to come back to the Lord and she promised she would try the local Elim church next Sunday. We left and I went home a really happy lady.

The news soon got around the village of how God had supplied me with a beautiful wedding dress. A friend of Mum's, Mrs Stone, said she would like to see the dress and if I was in agreement she would alter it in some way to make it more personal, so I wasn't wearing someone else's dress, but mine. She put a few darts in the bodice and it looked even better. When I went to collect it she asked if I noticed there was a small oil mark on the hem. Actually I hadn't and I don't think anyone else would have noticed it either.

Aunty Sheila was at home visiting Mum when I returned, so I asked her if she could see the mark. She found it eventually. 'Look,' she said, 'My friend owes me a favour, she works in the wardrobe department at the television studios, I'm sure she would know how to remove it.' So she contacted her friend who suggested we took it for her to see. She decided it would come out if it was cleaned and would send it to the cleaners for me.

To cut a long story short, it didn't come out but she had a friend who would sew satin around the length of the train to cover it. The dress came back looking a million dollars, and it didn't cost me a penny. Isn't God good?

Chapter 7

The Big Day

The summer passed by very quickly. The big day was fast approaching. We planned to have a small wedding with friends and family helping to provide a buffet reception. So many people promised to give different kinds of food for the buffet that Mum said, 'I hope the thirty-five people we have invited are really hungry.' By the time the 'Big day' came our thirty-five had risen to fifty-one. The actual number that arrived was eighty-three. So that was why God provided so much food, including the wedding cake.

A wedding cake, now that is important. I really hadn't a clue how much one would cost, but I knew God had provided so far and He wouldn't let us down now. So I talked to Him about it.

My aunty was visiting Mum again and the subject of the cake came up in conversation. Mum said, 'We haven't decided what to do about that yet.' So there and then it was decided that if we provided the ingredients, my aunty would have the cake made for a wedding present: but we would have to get someone to ice it. This sounded great, but we still needed the ingredients. It wasn't long before God started supplying them. My cousin Carole worked in an egg packing company, and her boss said she could have as many cracked eggs as she wanted free of charge. Someone else gave the fruit, another the flour and someone gave the margarine; all the ingredients arrived and the cake was made.

All we needed now was someone to ice it. A friend of a friend knew a lady who might do it, so my aunty approached her. It turned out that she knew my Mum and she could remember when I used to go 'spud bashing' (picking up potatoes) in the field behind her house. Yes, she would be delighted to do it for me, as a wedding present of course. Thank you Lord.

The whole reception cost my parents less than £10, and that was for the hire of the glasses and the non-alcoholic wine for the toast.

We had three bridesmaids: Faith, my friend from college, my niece Sonia and her friend, Sharon. Faith wanted to buy her own dress, so we just needed to dress the two little ones. Mum and I went into every shop in Southampton looking for dresses, but we couldn't find anything suitable. I was talking to Elsie Threlfall, a lady I worked with, about this and she said 'Don't worry, buy some material and bring me two of the children's dresses and I will make them for you.'

I was so excited, I couldn't wait to get home and tell Mum. We didn't have a telephone or I would have phoned her. I can still visualize Mum's face now, as she danced around the room saying 'Praise the Lord' when she heard of God's provision. The very next day Mum went into Southampton to buy the material. As always she prayed before she went. She decided to start at the top of the High Street and work her way down. The first shop was Tyrell and Greens, we didn't visit that shop very often because it was 'a posh shop'. I felt uncomfortable going in there because the pile on the carpet was so deep I was almost afraid of crushing it, or making it dirty.

Mum decided to go in and have a look. There was a big box of remnants so she thought she would look there first. As she was looking an assistant came and asked if she could help her. Mum explained what she wanted, and the assistant said 'I think I may have just what you are looking for.' She went away and came back with two remnants of brocade material the exact pattern of the wedding dress. It cost exactly £3 for two beautiful bridesmaid dresses. Thanks Elsie, and of course, thank you Lord.

I had everything I needed except shoes. Now shoes have always been a problem. It was bad enough when I took size 8, but now I needed size 9 with a wide fitting. I tried everywhere, and one sales assistant told me quite rudely, 'You don't need shoes Madam, you need canoes.' I wasn't in the mood for jokes, I needed shoes. At the next shop I was offered a pair of shoe boxes. So I decided to go home.

On the bus I felt I should get off at Totton and try in Chances shoe shop. A very friendly lady told me they didn't sell size 9, but she was sure I only needed size 8. I knew differently. I had been trying to squeeze my feet into size 8s all afternoon. 'Just a minute' she said as she disappeared into the back room. She came back with a lovely pair of white satin shoes, the exact shoes I was looking for, but they were size 8. 'Do try them,' she insisted, so I did, and to my utter amazement, they fitted like a glove. They were so comfortable I bought another pair of navy patent ones to wear with my 'going away suit'.

I wore the shoes for the wedding and the navy ones for the honeymoon, they were just so comfortable. When I got home Mum suggested maybe I should dye the satin shoes and wear them for best. As we were talking I thought I would just slip them on and decide what colour to have them dyed, but they wouldn't go on my feet. I tried and tried, but there was no way I could get my feet into those shoes. God had allowed my feet to shrink for that week so that I would have shoes for the wedding. He certainly moves in mysterious ways.

I thank God from the bottom of my heart for making our wedding such a wonderful occasion. It was certainly a marriage made in heaven, and now thirty-one years later Marcel and I are still very much in love, not only with each other, but also with God.

We have had lots of problems and difficulties just like any other couple, but praise God, as we have kept Him at the centre of our marriage He has brought us safely through.

Chapter 8

A Very Testing Time

Our week's honeymoon on the Isle of Wight over, we went to Wellow for the weekend, before moving to Belgium. The journey to the Continent was different from what I had expected. I thought we would have so much to talk about, our future plans, our new home or maybe just 'sweet nothings', but to my surprise and disappointment Marcel seemed to want to spend much of the time walking around the ship on his own, whilst I kept our seats and looked after the bags. He seemed very quiet but didn't want to talk about whatever it was that was troubling him.

We arrived at our new home feeling very tired and disappointed that the furniture we had ordered still hadn't arrived by bedtime. So our first romantic night in our new home was spent with me sleeping in a fold-up bed and Marcel sleeping (or rather, not sleeping) in an armchair.

The next morning we had an early delivery of our furniture. It came in packs ready to be assembled and we had to carry it all up three flights of stairs to our little apartment. Most of the day was taken up assembling it and unpacking and little housewifely tasks, like cooking and cleaning.

The following day I woke up thinking, 'This is our home,' and of course thanking the Lord for all His goodness. Little did I know that we were about to move to another apartment. Our landlord knocked on the door and asked if we would like to move to the ground floor where there was a bigger apartment which was now for rent? The rooms were much bigger and there was so much more light, so we agreed we would move. I'm sure we should have a place in the Guiness book of records for living for the shortest period in a rented apartment. So our second day was spent dismantling furniture, packing, moving and reassembling furniture again.

It would be great to be able to say this was the beginning of a wonderful carefree life, with God pouring out His blessings on us, pressed down and overflowing. But life isn't like that, we live in a real world.

This was the beginning of possibly the greatest test God has put us through so far. Marcel knew it was going to happen, that is why he behaved the way that he did on the ferry coming over. God told him what we would have to go through, and he was afraid to tell me, in case I took the next ferry back to England.

The heavenly supply seemed to stop, and there were times when we had no money, and often no food. We found an old, broken chair and broke it up to give us a little heat. The stove was not working properly and the only way to light it was to open the windows, light the stove, go out and close the door. When the smoke had stopped belching out from the window we knew it was safe to go back in, the stove would be alight.

When I said we had no food, I really meant no food. God seemed to supply either enough money for us to buy a 5 kilo bag of coal or a small loaf of bread. We usually ate just dry bread because we didn't have the money to buy anything to go on it. One day I had a real longing for an orange so instead of bread Marcel bought two oranges. We sliced them into quarters and that particular day we had four meals, we ate a quarter of an orange for each meal.

God was very gracious and kept us in good health and on a spiritual high throughout this time. He also sent the rent money in on the day it was due and the electricity bill was paid on time. Even if we received only £1 the first thing we did was to take out our tithe. Never say you can't afford to tithe, you can't afford not to.

One morning we woke up and actually decided to stay in bed to keep warm, we had no fuel for the fire, no food and it was snowing. So just for a laugh I asked Marcel what he would like for dinner. Between us we chose the soup, the main course, the sweet and we even decided to end with cheese and biscuits. I then got up, and Marcel was getting dressed when our door bell rang. Standing at the door was a friend of Marcel's from Holland. He was visiting a family in the next town, and had been sent over to invite us to join them for dinner. We were delighted, this was going to be our first meal for several weeks. We started with soup, (yes the one we had decided to have in our make-believe game). I gave Marcel a nudge and said 'I bet I know what we are having for the main course' and sure enough everything we had chosen was served up to us at that meal, even the cheese and biscuits.

A few days later we received a letter from Holland to say one of Marcel's friends was coming to stay for a few days and would be arriving that very same morning. We had no food or money, but managed to find some old wood under the stairs enough to light a fire. It was a very small fire, but it was all we had. I placed a kettle of water on top of the stove at 8.30 a.m. and it took until 12 noon to actually boil.

In the meantime Marcel's friend arrived. To my amazement he walked straight through the dining room into the kitchen and closed the door. I thought he must be using the toilet which was off the balcony through the kitchen. He came back having left his case in the kitchen. Marcel and I had agreed that if we had had food we would have shared it with him, but if we were fasting then he must share the fast with us as well. It was one thing saying it between ourselves, but I certainly wasn't going to tell him.

We sat talking and just before noon he suggested I go and prepare some food for lunch, so that was my opportunity to slip out into the kitchen and leave Marcel to explain that we had no food. As I walked into the kitchen I just couldn't believe my eyes. There on the top of my cupboard was a bread basket which had been empty for weeks, full of oranges, I counted them, there were twenty-four. I then opened the cupboard and it too was totally full of food. There was a lot of prepacked cooked meat, vegetables, bread, milk, cheese and coffee. We had a wonderful meal, in fact we were able to eat for many days from this wonderful gift.

Our troubles weren't over, for when the food ran out we had nothing again. A short time later I was looking out of the window and saw a red cabbage lying in the gutter. I certainly wasn't going to go out in the street and pick up that red cabbage, I hated red cabbage. Whilst I was standing there telling the Lord there was no way I was going to pick food out of the gutter, the lady from the basement apartment went out and picked it up.

It just seemed that God was seeing how far I was willing to go. After that things began to change and His provision began to flow again.

I must say during that period of about three months both Marcel and I were very aware of God's presence and felt 'high' spiritually. We still often laugh at the sight we must have been, sitting in our lounge in freezing temperatures dressed in jumpers, coats, dressing-gowns, gloves and scarves. When the door bell rang it was a mad rush to discard some of these layers before answering the door. If any of our visitors had looked behind the settee, they would have found a pile of clothes we had just discarded.

Chapter 9

Another Move

Marcel was asked if he would be willing to come over to Portsmouth and open a Bible School for International Gospel Outreach. After prayer we felt this was in God's will for us. I applied for a position as house-mother in a local children's home, as Marcel's was an unpaid position. I was called for an interview so we both travelled to Portsmouth and I was told immediately that I had been accepted for the post. This was great, I loved working with children.

My brother and brother-in-law offered to go over to Belgium and collect our furniture. We had already contacted the customs and they said we would have to pay duty on any furniture which was less than a year old. That meant most of it as we had only been married around nine months at the time.

Marcel decided to go back to Belgium and sort out the legal papers for the move whilst I stayed in England for a week and would travel over with my brother Dave, and show him the way to our home in Oostende.

When Marcel left for Belgium we were still in need of the money for the customs. I continued praying and a strange thing happened. On Wednesday every time I tried to pray I found myself thanking God for the money. So I assumed that Marcel had the money in Belgium. All the money I had was £7 and I needed to pay Dave's petrol money from that.

We travelled to Belgium on Saturday arriving in the evening and planned to leave on the 10 a.m. ferry on Sunday morning. So we loaded the truck with everything except the mattresses as we would need them for sleeping on.

It was late when we eventually lay down to sleep. This was the first opportunity Marcel and I had of talking to each other alone. 'Do you have the money for the customs?' I asked.

'No' he said sounding quite surprised, 'I thought you had it. Since Wednesday every time I have tried to pray for it I found myself praising God and thanking Him for the money,' the exact same thing that had happened to me.

Now I was really in a fix. Marcel was going on to Holland to translate for a team of English ministers and I was going back to England with an unsaved brother and brother-in-law with a load of furniture and no money to pay the customs. Oh, and there was also the freight duty to pay for the privilege of taking the truck through the port. Marcel had to leave at 7 a.m. and I was left with the problem. Dave and Ron would have thought me absolutely barmy if they had known the situation we were all in, so I didn't tell them, I just talked to the Lord.

In no time at all the White Cliffs of Dover were looming up before us, and I had to face the customs officer. I was feeling pretty scared. We had written out an honest list of all the items we had with us and I read and re-read it hundreds of times on our journey over. Now it was time to face the music.

Dave drove into the queue and was told there was absolutely no way we would be allowed to take freight through on a Sunday and he should go and park up in the compound until Monday. Dave was looking worried, he had to work on Monday. 'Stay where you are,' I said bravely, and as I said it another customs officer waved us to go to the desk. Dave drove over and I got out with my much read list.

The officer looked at me and looked at the list, then he went through each item and wrote little figures in red ink by each one. After what seemed an age, he asked if we had any cigarettes or spirits. I had the Holy Spirit, but I knew he didn't mean that, Ron had tobacco and Dave cigarettes so I told him. He stamped a card and said, 'Hand it in on the way out.' I just stood there so he repeated, 'Hand it in on the way out, you may go now.'

He didn't have to say that a second time, I jumped into the truck and we were out of the port in no time. I remember Dave saying, 'Bet you're glad that's over.' If only he knew how glad I really was.

As we drove very quickly along the dual carriageway, there was an old Bedford van in front of us. Its doors were tied on with rope, there was rope hanging from the exhaust pipe and it looked as if at any moment it would fall to pieces. Dave was driving very close to it and at quite high speed and I was definitely feeling a bit nervous, so I suggested we stop at a transport cafe and have a cup of tea.

We spent about half an hour in the cafe before continuing our drive to Portsmouth. After travelling around half an hour we came across a terrible accident, the Bedford van we had been following was completely wrecked. I often wonder if we would have been in that accident if we hadn't stopped for that cup of tea. Was this another occasion when God was protecting us from dangers seen and unseen?

As we arrived in Portsmouth I asked Dave how much I owed him for the petrol (remember I only had £7). Dave carefully worked it out. '£6. 17s. 6d.' he said. 'Here Dave,' I said, and handed him the £7; 'you can keep the change.'

By the way I had to turn down the job at the children's home because there was no one to cook for the students, so guess who ended up cooking again. I was very disappointed for I had been looking forward to having a salary again, but it seemed that God had other plans.

Chapter 10

Portsmouth

This was a strange but very different chapter in our lives. In Belgium, although Marcel had spent many hours every day in prayer we still had time to spend with each other. He was the only person I was able to speak to as I did not understand Flemish and very few people we knew spoke any English. But now in England we had moved into a house with another family, Bob and Anne Searle and their two children, the bible school students and what seemed like an endless supply of visitors. Suddenly I was only seeing Marcel when we all sat down to a meal with everybody else and late at night. He was either in classes, preparing and marking work or helping the students. I just seemed to be the one who did all the cooking, housework and shopping and I found it a very lonely existence. After a while I decided things had to change, so we made a ruling that the students would be responsible for clearing up after lunch and Marcel and I would spend half an hour together (alone!) before the afternoon session of lessons or outreach would begin. In theory it worked, but in practice there was always an emergency that just had to be attended to. This was a very difficult time for me. A decision was then made without my knowing that it would save a lot on the expenses if Bob, Ann and the children had their midday meal with us. It was great for everyone except me. I didn't have any transport and I had more shopping to carry and cook. So it wasn't all easy, in fact I think it was probably the hardest year of my life.

During this time Bob invited a family over from Holland to stay for a holiday. That was fine, they were a lovely family, but on the day before their arrival he informed us that he was going to a conference in London and we could meet them and look after them.

'Lord help!' We were short of pillows and short of food. That night we were having our evening prayer time with the students before going to bed, when our doorbell rang. There standing on the door step was my sister with a very large parcel in her hands. 'Mum said she was trying to turn the big feather mattress this morning when God told her you needed some pillows today, I don't know what she is on about, but here are the pillows.' Inside the parcel was a note saying how she was finding the mattress so heavy to turn, so she prayed and asked God to help her, it was then that He had told her about my urgent need for pillows. Mum had some ticking in the house, so she made the pillows. Apparently someone came to her door when she was filling the pillows and she said she had so many feathers in her hair she didn't know whether she should cackle or say hello. Thank you Lord, we now had pillows.

The family were coming in time for tea, and the only food I had in the house was a bag of potatoes. So I decided I would make chips. Well the family arrived and it was time to get tea, the students were all out doing outreach. The little boy kept asking 'What are we going to have for tea?'

I said, 'It's going to be a surprise.'

As I began peeling the potatoes and chipping them, he grew quite excited. 'I know, I know,' he shouted, 'we are going to have chips.'

'That's right, we are going to have chips.'

'What are we going to have with our chips?' he asked.

'I told you it's going to be a surprise.' That was the absolute truth, I had no idea what we would be eating with our chips.

The students began returning from their outreach, and Daniel came struggling in with a big box. 'Whatever do you have there?' I asked.

'Something really strange happened to me whilst I was walking home,' he said. 'As I was walking past the supermarket, the more I tried to walk forward, the more I kept finding myself walking backwards, then I found myself walking through the door pushing a trolley. I had no idea what I was doing there, so I walked down the aisles and found myself placing all sorts of things into the trolley, and here they are.'

Thank you Lord, right on time again. We had ham, eggs and chips and there was even cake in the box too. I really love surprises, but they can be a bit scary especially when I'm responsible for feeding a number of people knowing the cupboard is bare.

On another occasion our doorbell went late at night. It was Arthur Burt and five other people who had just missed the last boat to the Isle of Wight. Please could they stay the night with us. Of course that was no problem. The difficulty came at breakfast the next morning; we had plenty of food but I only had half a pint of milk. There was a dairy on the other side of the road, but I didn't have the money to buy any. When we had a need we only told the Lord. I'm sure if Arthur knew we needed milk he would have willingly bought us some.

So there I was preparing breakfast and telling the Lord of our need. Now I don't know if you are anything like me, but there are occasions when I also try to tell the Lord how He could meet the need. If everybody had toast instead of cereals, and also had black tea or coffee our need would be met.

As I was thinking this, I suddenly remembered the story in the bible of the woman's cruse of oil that just kept on pouring out. 'That's it Lord, you did it for her so you can do it for me.'

Everyone sat down to breakfast, I'm not sure if there were seventeen or nineteen of us, and the much prayed over half pint of milk was carefully placed in the middle of the table. To my horror, everyone had cereals, and my heart kept missing a beat as I watched the cornflakes floating in the dishes, which seemed full of milk. Then everyone had one or two cups of tea or coffee, all taking milk.

At the end of breakfast there was still milk over. It was quite a long time before I shared this miracle with anyone, I felt they would all think I was a headcase and wouldn't believe it. Then I was in a meeting where the preacher said, 'A blessing isn't a blessing until it is shared.' Since that time I have shared this blessing on many occasions.

Chapter 11

Fantastic Memories

This is how I can best describe the time we spent in Southern Ireland. We moved here after living in Havant and Northern Ireland.

We spent some time in a little church in Dublin where we have some very happy memories. I think maybe the open air meetings in O'Connell Street will stay in my memory until the day I die. Each Saturday evening and Sunday afternoon we were there witnessing and giving out tracts that we had printed ourselves.

One particular Saturday evening I remember talking to a man about the Lord and he said, 'If you only knew where I had been and what I have been doing today you would never speak to me.' I remember saying, 'God knows everything about you and He still loves you.'

He seemed a little taken aback and he opened his jacket and a gun fell to the ground. 'I've used this gun to kill people this weekend,' he said. 'God knows all about that too,' I answered. We talked for a while and he went away with some literature.

Another day as I was singing a solo 'How Great Thou Art' a man pushed through the crowd and stood immediately in front of me. I kept singing, then he began to throw punches directly at my face. As the punches neared me there was a loud noise as if he was hitting a piece of metal, and it was obviously very painful for him. He looked at his fist, then tried again and repeated this action several times before going away in a very bewildered state. The Lord gave me the ability to keep singing. I am totally convinced that God placed a protective barrier between me and this man. Others in the group all heard the bang as he threw the punches.

We also had a Sunday school and the Legion of Mary used to send children in to disrupt the class. One little boy was so badly behaved one week that I made him leave. He begged me to let him stay, but I said no, if he promised to behave he could come back the next week. When he came the following week he told me that he was in terrible trouble with the Legion of Mary and they had given him a whole list of questions to ask me so that I would not be able to teach the lesson. I was able to use some of the questions in my lesson and gave bible verses to prove my answers, and the little boy learned them all by heart. It was a great way of teaching him and the other children bible verses to prove what we believed and the little boy took the verses back to the Legion of Mary. After a few weeks the Legion of Mary stopped sending the children and in fact they were banned from coming, but they still came to talk to me at the open-air meeting.

We then went to live in Tramore where I worked as 'Lady Superintendent' of the YWCA Holiday Home. This title sounds rather grand, but actually I was still 'Plain Jen and no nonsense.'

At the holiday home I had some very nice young girls working for me. They were usually around 14 years old and were excellent workers. We had some terrific times together, and were more of a family than workers.

Each morning I was responsible for 'Doing Prayers,' I tried to make the short talk light and relevant to the people's needs. Most days after prayers there was a queue of people outside my office door asking for prayer or just wanting to know more about salvation, baptism in water or the baptism in the Holy Spirit.

Most weeks I had the joy of leading guests to the Lord, some went home baptized in water (in the sea) and others baptized in the Holy Spirit. It was a time of really great blessing.

During this time Marcel and I were invited to a meeting of young people who had all got saved in various places during their summer holidays. When they returned home they found that their friends had all had a similar experience. They began meeting by the side of the road to have communion together, then one of them found an old condemned flat in Johnstown. It was over a fish shop, the back yard was full of old fish heads and the rats, flies, stray dogs and all that goes with them.

The stairs had several boards missing and the bathroom floor was almost non-existent, it was necessary to balance on the beams where the boards were missing to get to the toilet. As you can imagine it was only used in absolute emergencies. The other rooms were a little safer. It was to a meeting at this flat we were invited.

The meeting was held in the kitchen, where young people with very long hair and quite scruffy appearances were sitting on broken chairs, the table, the draining boards, the cooker, the floor and some standing. Two vacated their seats for us. I remember praying a quick prayer that the chair wouldn't collapse and that I wouldn't go home with fleas. I must admit it was quite an experience.

As soon as the meeting started I forgot all my fears for these young people who had only been saved for a short time were really on fire spiritually. I was so blessed but I'm afraid Marcel wasn't! When we went home he said 'Never again. If you want to go that's fine, but no way am I going back there.' It sounded very final.

Well I just prayed. I could see such tremendous potential in these young people and really felt it was right to help them.

The following Friday, every time Marcel tried to pray he began to cry, in fact he cried most of the day. God was dealing with him and gave him such a love for these folk. Guess who was at the meeting the following Sunday? Yes, God had truly broken Marcel and he was able to see beyond the outward appearance and the disgusting flat.

We had many wonderful times in that flat and all of the young people were baptized in both water and the Holy Spirit. They were so keen to learn and testify. At one point we decided to have one night a week off, so that we could have some time to ourselves but also so that the young ones could spend time in their own homes testifying. It never worked, there was always an emergency or a question that just had to be answered immediately, so we very rarely had an evening to ourselves. All the other evenings were taken up with prayer meetings, bible studies and outreach. They were so keen to learn and share what they had learned.

We had some very difficult times doing outreach. One evening two of the boys were beaten up and as we left the place in a borrowed van, we were stoned. Many stones hit the van, but praise God no damage was done.

On another occasion, when I was driving to collect two of the people for a meeting as their motor bike had broken down, a man stood in the middle of the road on a hairpin bend. I had to stop the car. My window was down and he drew a gun holding it a short distance from my face and said, 'If I ever see you in the place again I will blow your head off.'

'Well if you do,' I said, 'I know I will be going to heaven, how about you?' Don't misunderstand me, I'm not ultra brave, but I believe that that was God speaking through me. He made no comment and I continued to make regular visits to that area.

All of the young people were Roman Catholics and left the Church the moment God showed them 'the truth of salvation'. This made the priests very angry and they did all they could to frustrate the work from going ahead. They regularly hammered notices to the door of the flat, saying that this was a dangerous building and no one should enter. When this didn't stop the young folk from coming into the meetings, they used to send 'plainclothes' priests to the meetings. On one such occasion we were having a really blessed time and two of the girls asked if we would pray for them to receive the baptism of the Holy Spirit. We prayed and they both began to praise the Lord in tongues at which the poor priest looked totally petrified. He jumped from his seat and ran down the stairs and he never bothered us again.

I must admit that one evening I actually felt seasick in a prayer meeting. It was a very wet and windy evening and the wind was blowing through the floor boards making the lino move up and down. Although I kept my feet very firmly on the floor the lino continued to move and the continuous movement made me feel quite unwell.

We had a rat in the flat too, we called him Fred. I was very aware of something brushing my leg during a prayer time. I opened my eyes and there was an enormous rat which immediately ran under a settee where three of the girls were sitting. I just prayed (with one eye open) that it wouldn't come out during the service, thankfully it didn't.

A little later someone lit a fire in the kitchen fireplace, not knowing that Fred was up the chimney. That evening when we arrived at the flat there was a note on the table, written on a sheet of white cardboard with a thick black outline, saying, 'Fred is dead'.

We had some very precious times in that condemned flat and lives were truly changed by the power of God. It was never necessary to ask the young ones to tidy themselves up for as they began to grow spiritually their appearance began to change. I guess this is a very important lesson for us all to learn. Lasting change only comes from the inside. Changing one's hair style, clothes and habits because one is told one should will not last, but if we allow God to change the heart, then the other things will follow.

The time came when we had to move out of the flat, and God provided us with a suitable place at 3, Scotch Quay. This meant that the rent was much higher and we needed extra money. All of the young people were very faithful in paying their tithes. So I prayed asking the Lord to give each of them a rise, so that the extra tithes would meet the bills. I didn't tell them of my prayer, only Marcel knew.

The next day, Monday, one of the lads arrived at our door really excited, 'Guess what, the boss gave me a rise today.' Shortly after another one came, 'I've been promoted to supervisor and been given a rise.' The third one had been promoted to quality controller and he too had a rise. Before the evening was over all of them had come to share the news that they had received a rise in their wages. Isn't God good? If we are faithful to Him He will provide all of our needs.

I am so thankful to God for the privilege of being able to work with Him in Southern Ireland. The work was very hard, but so rewarding.

Chapter 12

Practise the Presence of the Lord

After spending a number of years in Ireland we returned to my home village in southern England. We were both very tired and in need of a spiritual break, so we felt it was right to do some secular work for a while and use the money to support others who were working full-time for the Lord.

My father had a driving school and he desperately wanted me to work with him. I hadn't any idea about teaching driving, but to keep him happy I decided I would take the necessary examinations and if I passed I would work with him. To my utter amazement I passed and really enjoyed the work. I had so many opportunities to witness.

On one occasion I was teaching a young woman how to reverse around a corner. She had great difficulty straightening the car once she had turned the corner. In the back window I had a text 'We have peace with God through our Lord Jesus Christ' so I suggested she lined the kerb up with one of the letters from the text, then she would know how far she was from the kerb. She tried it a couple of times without success, then she shouted 'I've got it, I've got it, if I keep right in the centre of Jesus Christ I'll be alright!' Guess who had more than just a driving lesson on the way home?

Another person was getting very worked up about their three-point turn. Being a Christian, I suggested that maybe we should stop by the side of the road and pray about it. We did and within a short while they mastered the manoeuvre.

I was taking a young man in for his test who was very nervous as most of his friends had passed first time. He came from a Christian home, but was not a believer himself. As we were driving towards the test centre an examiner passed us and waved, and I said, 'Oh he is a very nice guy, he is a Christian.' The lad immediately said, 'Do you think if I asked God he would let me have him as my examiner?' 'Why do you want him?' I asked. 'Well if he is a Christian I know I will get a fair test, because Christians are honest people.' A few moments later he asked, 'Do you think if I asked God He would let me pass my test?' 'Maybe,' I said. 'Can we stop and pray then?' he said. (At that point I really wished his mother and father could have heard our conversation.) 'Of course we can.' I said. So we found a safe place and stopped the car. I let him pray quietly to himself, then we travelled on to the test centre.

The examiners came out, and sure enough the Christian called out my pupil's name. His face was a picture, he just beamed at me as he walked out of the waiting room. When he came back he was told he had passed, he was so excited. On the way home I stopped the car and said to the lad, 'Boy have you got a problem now.' 'Why, why?' he asked anxiously. 'Well you prayed and God has just answered your prayer hasn't He?' 'Yes, but why is that a problem?' he asked. 'You have just proven there is a God, so what are you going to do about it?' He didn't talk much on the way home, but I prayed a lot for him.

One Christian lady went in for her test and failed, she was so miserable. I quoted a few verses to her like 'Praise the Lord in all things,' and 'All things do work together for good.' Now I could understand her disappointment, but it is strange how some people can only praise the Lord when they are getting their own way and everything is going well for them. I think Mum used to call them 'Fair weather Christians.'

Apart from the driving school I also taught in the local Sunday school. I always prayed much about the lessons and the songs that we would sing. One morning as I prayed I felt the Lord was saying 'Practise the presence of the Lord' I began questioning Him how I could do this with young children, whose ages ranged from four to fourteen. The chorus 'I just want to praise you, lift my hands and say I love you.' kept going through my mind. So when I got to the church I asked the minister's wife if she could play it. She really didn't think it was appropriate, but after I explained why I was going to use it, she understood. Firstly I went through the words with the children explaining what they meant, and getting suggestions from them as to why we should love Jesus.

We sang it through a couple of times and there was such an anointing in the place. I asked the children if they felt anything whilst we were singing, and one little boy said, 'It's like a quiet feeling.' Another said, 'It's sort of peaceful.' The little four-year old said, 'It's nice.' They all wanted to sing it again, so I explained that the nice, quiet, peaceful feeling was God's presence. He was showing us that He was here with us and wanted to help us. So before singing it again we prayed for things the children wanted to pray for. We asked God to make one little girl's knee better because she had fallen over, and one little boy's rabbit better and another child's Granny better. Then we sang again and this time without me saying anything, they all closed their eyes and raised their hands. It was beautiful. We sang it many times before the end of the meeting and then every Sunday the children would ask for it. So please don't limit the children's ability to experience God's presence. I love working with children, their faith is so simple.

Later whilst teaching in another Sunday school in Salisbury, the topic was 'being born again,' so at the end of the lesson I asked if any of the children there were born again. One child half raised her hand, I'm half born again,' she said. 'That's great,' I said. 'Tell us how you became half born again.' 'I asked Jesus into my heart,' she said, 'but I didn't know I had to say sorry for all the wrong things I've done.' So before the class was over she did it properly, and was fully born again. She is now a fine young lady and is really going on with the Lord.

The Lord opened the way for Marcel to pastor again in the north of England. Our home was about eight miles from the church and I felt the Lord would have me to open a children's meeting in our home. It is very difficult when you are new to an area and you don't have any children of your own, to actually approach children without people suspecting you of being odd! So first of all we got to know our neighbours very well and their four children. The children were always in our house, so I suggested to them one day that maybe we could have a children's meeting. They all agreed to this. At the first meeting they asked lots of questions about heaven and hell and I gave them honest answers and told them how they could be sure of going to heaven. The next day my doorbell didn't stop ringing. One of the boys had spent all day telling his friends about Jesus and none of them wanted to go to hell, so he kept bringing them round for me to tell them how to get to heaven.

This was the start of a super children's meeting. Our weekly meeting soon grew to twenty-two children, although most of them came to our house every evening. They finished school around 3 p.m. and from about 3.45 p.m. they would start knocking the door to see if they could come in yet. I had to make a rule that they must wait until we had our meal which was usually around 6 p.m. By then there was quite a long queue outside our gate waiting for me to say they could come in. Most evenings we played games (Uno was a firm favourite) and we made countless paper-mâché models. There were times when I had lines of piggy-banks or masks hanging in my kitchen to dry. One young boy was very good at making lighthouses with a light that flashed and would spend hours fiddling around with a battery, wires and a bulb. Sometimes we would just talk or do their homework together. I am afraid Marcel found it all a bit much and would disappear to his study until it was time to make coffee.

I remember one Sunday some of the lads came to church with us and they were interested to know why people raised their hands when they were singing and praying. I explained that they were just submitting themselves to God. One boy asked if the ones who only raised one hand were only half submitted to God? I will leave you to think about that one.

Later Marcel was ill and had to leave the church where he was pastor so we attended a local church. The children were delighted by this because it now meant that they could all come with us to church. Before we could only take as many as we could squeeze into the back of our mini car. So some of the children would come to our house and walk with us, others would join us as we passed their homes. One lady told me we looked like the Pied Piper every Sunday as the children ran and skipped along the road with us to church. I guess we did look a bit of a sight, but a very happy sight. We really enjoyed sharing the Lord with the folk there, especially the children.

It wasn't all easy, but the Lord was very gracious to us. I remember one morning a thought kept coming into my mind. It was 'Try the spirits to see if they are from God.' I didn't know what it was referring to, but in the evening our doorbell went and an elderly lady was standing on the step with a rather large bag. I'd never seen her before, but she said, 'God has told me to come and live with you and be your church evangelist. 'That's funny,' I said, 'I was talking to Him just now and He didn't tell me anything about it.' Needless to say we didn't allow her to stay, but we must take heed of God's warnings, and we must keep very close to Him so that we can hear what He is saying to us.

There are always people ready to use you, especially if they see that you have a caring heart; so take care, if the devil can distract you from God's perfect will, he will. And remember, he often comes in sheep's clothing.

Chapter 13

Our Greatest Challenge So Far

We moved south again and Marcel was soon well enough to take over another pastorate. This was a completely different situation from any we had ever come across before. Our previous churches were very young churches, in the sense that the people were young and all very keen to go on with the Lord. This church was about forty years old and had already had several splits. Now there was just a handful of people left and a lot of 'baggage' from the past. There had not been a pastor for a number of months and the church was very disjointed when we arrived. After a while everything seemed to be going well and some gypsies from the area who had accepted the Lord whilst they were 'on the road' returned home and came to the church.

This gave us an opening into the gypsy camp and many more gypsies began coming and finding the Lord. We started a children's meeting and many of the children were from the camp. Now you would think the folk at the church would be happy to see all of these gypsies coming to the meetings. Of course they weren't used to church and didn't always behave in the way we did, but they were coming and hearing the gospel and God was changing lives.

Then the complaints started. We should tell the gypsies it was a sin to go to the shop on Sunday. (Those who complained had houses and fridges and didn't need to buy milk and bread every day.) Most of the gypsies who came to church smoked. People complained that this made their clothes smell as if they had been in a pub when they sat near them and it was very embarrassing because people they met may have thought that they smoked. Often after the meeting before having a cup of tea, some would go out in the road and have a cigarette. Then they would lean on the church fence talking and throw their cigarette ends onto the pavement. I used to go out and brush them up after everyone had gone home. As pastors, the complainers said, it was our place to tell them that smoking was a sin and they shouldn't smoke anywhere near the church. The complaints continued. I didn't once hear anybody pray thanking the Lord for the privilege of having these folk in the church or for the opportunity of sharing the gospel with them.

Of course Marcel's sermons had to be made simpler because many of our new congregation had difficulty reading and needed to be fed on the milk of the word. This caused yet more complaints from those who came to the church to be fed and needed the meat of the word.

As the work with the gypsies grew, some of the congregation who should have been helping with the teaching left the church. So the extra workload was placed on Marcel and myself. We had folk coming to our house every day for teaching and prayer and we had all the meetings to prepare for as well. After every meeting there was always a queue of people wanting prayer for problems, sickness or the baptism of the Holy Spirit. The older people in the church all made excuses that they had to get away early and we were often still there ministering after 10 p.m.

One Sunday I committed the unforgivable sin. So many gypsies came that we ran out of milk, and I went to the shop and bought some more. I don't think I was ever totally forgiven for doing such a thing. More people left. We had a lot of baptismal services too but it was usually left to Marcel and I to prepare and heat the pool and also empty it. Later we received help from some of the new Christians.

One gypsy lady came to me and asked if she could be baptized. I said 'No because you are living in sin.' She laughed. 'But I've been living in sin for fifty-two years,' she said. 'Then you have been sinning for a very long time and that doesn't make it right,' I said. A couple of days later she asked if we would go to her wedding at the registry office and then could she please be baptized. I will never forget their wedding. Her husband was dancing down the stairs swinging his walking stick and as excited as any newly-wed person I have ever seen.

At one time we had a gypsy mission in the church, it was a tremendous time and more local gypsies started coming to the meetings.

On another occasion they had a tent mission but used our church for the baptismal service. We said that they could only allow a hundred people in the church because of fire regulations. At least two hundred turned up, they were sitting anywhere they could find space and those who couldn't get in were standing on chairs leaning in the windows trying to see the service. I really wished I had a camera with me. Mind you, someone phoned the police because they couldn't understand what was going on, but by the time they arrived everyone had left and gone to an open-air service in the centre of Southampton.

We have some wonderful friends (and Christian brothers and sisters amongst the gypsy community) so please if God allows you to minister to them count it a great privilege and please remember to let God do the changing from the inside. Don't lay so many rules down that you frighten them away without even giving them the chance to hear and receive the gospel.

I must share one experience I had at the children's meeting. One little gypsy boy came running in begging me to talk to his sister. 'I got born again last night around the camp fire and if my sister don't get born again and the Lord comes back she will go to 'ell.'

His sister came in behind him and she didn't know what born again was anyway. So I explained it to her, and minutes later they were both on their knees as she repented and accepted the Lord. It was a real joy to see the changes taking place in their lives.

Not all are going on with the Lord, but at least they know the truth. The seed has been planted and in time I believe that God will bring forth fruit in their lives.

We didn't only work with gypsies, God brought three Christadelphians in to the church. They got wonderfully saved and led many of their friends and families to the Lord. We had a great bonfire as we burned all their books and studies. God wonderfully set them free from the wrong doctrines they had been taught and led them into his glorious light. Two of them had also been Jehovah's Witnesses in their search for the truth.

I always find it sad that people who are searching for the truth often seem attracted to false teachings. Are we failing as a Christian Church to openly share the gospel with those around us?

Altogether we spent seven years ministering in this church and I feel it was the hardest place the Lord has ever called us to minister. Before we had worked with people who had a tremendous desire to go on with the Lord and to share with others, but here it was as if some of the older people really didn't want anyone to come in and change their 'Little Church'. They certainly didn't want wicked people who drank, smoked and dared to go to the shop on a Sunday. There was no way they were going to get too close to any of them, they might catch something.

I particularly remember one Christmas when one of the older men who had a position in the church, asked me to write down the names of the people in the church so he could send them cards. They had been coming for a year and he didn't even know their names. I am afraid this lack of love was soon felt by everyone and it became a constant battle ground between the older and the newer Christians. When the newer ones began using the spiritual gifts, a real spirit of jealousy was revealed and often we could cut the atmosphere with a knife. Instead of thanking God for what He was doing in their lives, some would only recall what terrible people they were before they became Christians. I remember one person complaining to me that we shouldn't allow certain people to testify when they still went to the shop on Sunday.

We did our best to make excuses for the attitudes of some of the older folk, but we lost quite a few of the new people because of them. Thankfully many of them went to other churches, but some have gone away from the Lord. We still have contact with some of them and are able to encourage them to go on with the Lord.

It was very hard to understand why our greatest opposition came from within the church. We had people in our home most days for prayer and teaching, others were always on the phone or we were visiting them in their own homes. We always tried to make ourselves available to people and before God we tried to always give of our best, but there seemed to be a constant opposition. It may seem a very strange thing to say, but I feel we were both very relieved when God showed us it was time to move on.

We do miss many of our 'sheep' but we are very thankful for the phone calls and letters we receive regularly from them. In fact some of the gypsies have nicknamed me 'Mother Hen.' I don't mind, I will always try to make myself available to help them as long as they need me.

Chapter 14

Lord Sell A Whole Herd Of Cows

As we have continued in the ministry our faith has needed to grow quite dramatically. We are now in a situation where we are trusting the Lord for every cent of our own living and the needs of the work. 'Selling a cow,' has now changed to 'Lord, sell a whole herd of cows.'

In 1967 the Lord gave Marcel a vision whilst he was ministering in Ireland. It was of a 'home of prayer,' where ministers and Christian workers could come for a time of refreshing. It would be a place where they could just relax and wait on the Lord or receive ministry if needed.

Since receiving the vision we always opened our home to those who needed ministry. We have always believed that one of the most important qualities of a minister is availability in a relaxed homely atmosphere. I am afraid we have been misunderstood by ministers on many occasions who have thought that we were lowering the standard of the profession, by having such a relationship with our 'sheep'. But this is the ministry God has called US to.

The vision God gave Marcel in 1967 never left us and we kept it before us over the years, often reminding the Lord that we were getting older and if He didn't hurry up we would be too old to see its fulfilment. I guess at times we felt a bit like poor Moses waiting to arrive at the promised land.

A number of times the Lord has let us know that He hadn't forgotten the vision. One such time we were in a prayer meeting in a house in Rickleton, Tyne and Wear. A lady had a vision of Marcel and I with the word 'MINARET' written over our heads. She didn't know what this word was and just spelt out the letters to us. At the time we felt God was reminding us of the Home of Prayer since a minaret is the tower on the mosque where folk are called to prayer.

Shortly after this we were ministering in Holdbrook, Walthamstow, when another person had a vision of Marcel standing, praying wearing a prayer shawl and a skull cap. Since Marcel first became a Christian the Lord gave him a real love for the Jewish people and he felt that this vision was that God was saying the Home of Prayer would include the Jews in some way.

As we continued to pray about the Home of Prayer, God gave us the name 'Oasis of Peace' then He gave us in more detail what the purpose would be. Firstly prayer, then intercession, refuge and reconciliation. At this time we still had no idea where this home would be and I guess we assumed it would be somewhere in England.

This all changed in January 1995. It was my fiftieth birthday and Marcel really wanted to make it special for me, so he booked a holiday in Cyprus. Whilst in Cyprus we decided to visit Larnaca and see the Church of Lazarus. It is said that after Lazarus was raised from the dead that the Jews persecuted him and he fled to Cyprus and is supposed to be buried in this church.

At this time I was suffering from a neck problem and if I looked up or made any quick movement with my neck I would black out. As we walked along the very narrow street leading to the church, I suddenly looked up, and there towering above me was a minaret. Amazingly, I did not pass out.

Suddenly the vision came flooding back to me, I very excitedly shared it with Marcel. We both immediately felt that the Home of Prayer would be in Cyprus. But where would this fit in with our love for the Jewish people? We went back to our holiday apartment in Ayia Napa with our heads buzzing with questions.

It was only when we decided to look at the 'Air Tours' holiday folder that we realised there are ferries going from Limossol to Israel and there are daily flights from Larnaca airport. We have since found out that flights also go from Paphos. So it would be very easy for us to visit Israel and for folk to travel across to visit us. Also being placed just outside of Israel we would be close enough to keep in touch with what was happening and be able to listen to their news broadcasts, so have up-to-date fuel for prayer.

We went home from our holiday bubbling with excitement and with endless questions buzzing around in our heads. The hardest thing about it was that we could not share the news with anybody. Since Marcel was the pastor of a church, it would just unsettle people if we announced one day, that sometime in the future we would be moving to Cyprus. We needed to know more from God about the timing etc.

If only Mum was alive we could have shared it with her knowing she would not tell anybody, but sadly for us, she went home to be with the Lord nine months earlier. I knew that she would have been really excited and would have encouraged us in every way.

For the next few months excitement, doubts and fears filled our minds. I was far from healthy, Marcel has diabetes. There were many questions to be answered. How would we cope with the heat? Could we get the insulin in Cyprus? What if one of us became ill or died, how would the other one cope? Where would we get support? Being a pastor for the last seven years meant we were unable to visit other churches and lost contact with a lot of our friends. What about Dad? He was ill and had just lost Mum, his wife for almost sixty years. How would he react to us moving so far away?

We would have to give up our rented home and get rid of most of our belongings. We had done this on a number of occasions during our lifetime, but somehow this time it was harder. Marcel was in his early sixties and I was sick. In the natural it didn't seem wise to burn all of our bridges and go so far away with no security, no regular wage.

Yet we knew in our hearts that this was what God was calling us to do. It wasn't easy, but nowhere does God promise us an easy road. We came to the place where we were willing to go anywhere God wanted us to go, believing Him to supply all of our needs.

In December of the same year God made it possible for us to return to Cyprus for another holiday. We had no doubt in our minds that this really was the place God was calling us to. During our stay we gleaned as much information as we could about costs of living, housing, and requirements for obtaining an extension visa to live there. It came as a bit of a shock to find out that we would have to have at least £9,000

Cyprus pounds in a bank here before we would be given a visa to stay. Where were we going to get £9,000, which was then about £10,500 sterling? So the day before we returned home from our holiday, we prayed and asked the Lord to confirm this call by sending us a financial gift to open a 'Cyprus Ministries' account. When we arrived home the next day there was a letter from a missionary on our door mat. It contained a cheque for £65 with a note 'for whatever project you have in mind.' That letter must have been posted several days before we prayed that prayer. How could we doubt God's calling?

Chapter 15

Another Time Of Testing

The church we were pastoring had a business meeting every six months, so we decided we would wait until the March meeting before telling the church and giving them the required three months' notice. In the meantime we shared our intentions with a few very close friends whom we knew would pray for us. Between December and the business meeting in March we had received £1,000 in gifts, each one accompanied with a note or letter saying we were to use the monies for whatever project we had in mind, or words to that effect. Remember we hadn't shared the vision at this point.

March came and we told the church. Now we had made it known we could get people to pray and organise some meetings to raise the necessary support. The next thing was to send out a prayer letter, which we did with very little response. I don't think we even covered the cost of the letter or the postage.

So we sent out fifty-four letters to ministers asking if we could go and share the vision. We had three replies. One for a meeting locally in Rossmore, one in Chester-le-Street (County Durham) and one in Sunderland (Tyne & Wear). 'Lord what should we do?' we prayed. 'If we travel by train it will cost us about £100 each, if we go by coach it will cost us around £40 each. It wouldn't be right to cancel after they have offered us meetings.'

Whilst we were discussing what to do a leaflet was pushed through our door from the National Express Coach company. The special discount card which was available for the over 55s was now available for the over 50s (that meant me!). This would mean a saving of up to 30% on all journeys taken throughout the year. The cost of the card was £6 for a year. I turned the leaflet over to find another offer, for a limited period card holders could travel anywhere in the country for, I think, £6.99 return. The dates included the time we were due to speak in the North. Praise God He was answering our prayer, we would be able to go after all.

Sad to say, only one other minister bothered to reply, his church was busy with the Alpha course so it would be difficult to fit us in at this time.

This meant we had to rely solely on God for our provision. I know that is the way it should be, but I guess we all feel at times that we must give God a hand and help Him!

For years missionaries have had to raise all their support before being allowed to go to the field. In fact I have known of some very good dedicated people who have never reached the mission field because they could not satisfy the mission board of their guaranteed support. Not everyone has the dedication of Gladys Aylwood, who worked and saved for her fare when the missions board turned her down.

So there we were with the time quickly passing and no more meetings booked. Gifts were coming in very slowly, usually gifts of under £10. We appreciated every one and truly thanked God for each of them. But it takes a very long time to reach £100 and we needed a lot more than that. One day Marcel got quite cross with the Lord and told Him He would have to do better than that if we were ever going to make it. The next day we received an anonymous gift of £1,000.

The total was gradually rising but we did not have enough money by the time our notice ran out at the church. The church voted unanimously for us to stay for a further six months. Secretly I was very pleased we had to wait because I was praying 'Please Lord let us move in the winter so I can gradually get used to the heat.' It may sound selfish of me, but those who know me will tell you I am always hot.

Chapter 16

The Red Sea Experience

During this time of waiting I went through many very mixed emotions. I could be on a real 'spiritual high' one day and then the next day I would be questioning God if this really was His will. On one such occasion I was sitting in church supposedly listening to Marcel's sermon, and I was asking the Lord, 'Is it really Cyprus or have we got it wrong?' As I thumbed through my Bible I felt drawn to read Acts 13 v.4. The last line reads 'they sailed to Cyprus' I had a little laugh to myself and whispered to the Lord that it was good He hadn't called us to a place not mentioned in the Bible.

During this time God used the Children of Israel's journey from Egypt to speak many truths to me. In lots of ways we were experiencing similar things.

Marcel and I met a man in Totton and he wanted to know when we would be leaving for Cyprus. We told him that as soon as we had the money we were ready to go. He replied, 'God won't provide the boat until you get to the water'. That was true, but when the country was asking for the money up front it was difficult to give up your home and your possessions without seeing the money there. Maybe that may have seemed like lack of faith on our part, but we felt that God was well able to meet the need before we went.

One of the problems we faced was we seemed to be putting our faith in the post. Every day our spirits would rise or fall according to the amount of money we received in the mail. Then I read in the bible where the Children of Israel were placed in a very difficult situation. Their leader Moses in whom they trusted was leading them along the way, when he told them he had a word from the Lord. In Exodus 14 v.2

they were told that they should turn back (go back the way they came) and camp by the sea.

Next thing they heard was Pharaoh's army approaching. They were trapped with the sea in front of them and the army behind them.

In this terrible situation, what did Moses say? 'Fear not, stand still' You can almost hear them thinking, 'Is this man crazy or what? "Stand still" he says, we have no choice, the sea is in front of us, the army behind us, we have nowhere to go.' Now they have decided he must be totally crazy, he is telling them to go forward. Does he want them all to drown, doesn't he know they can't all swim?

Oh, no, what's happening? The angel of God and the pillar of the cloud were having none of this, they have gone behind the Israelites (v.19). 'God, what is happening?'

Where was Moses? Oh there, on the shore line with his rod in his hand stretching it out over the sea. Then a strong easterly wind started blowing, in fact it blew all night. The sea began to part and by morning there was a big wide dry path, the waters banked up on either side. The Children of Israel were able to pass through safely on dry ground.

Then I noted in the story that when it was morning Moses lifted his rod again to close the sea and all the Egyptians were drowned. God allowed them to actually see the destruction of their enemy.

Well here we were and I felt as if in our situation we too were trapped by the Red Sea. God was saying 'Go forward' and we still didn't have enough money. Our way ahead seemed blocked.

I went to the Ladies' Praise meeting feeling a bit down spiritually. At the end of the meeting I went forward for prayer, I just felt I needed a spiritual boost. As Mary prayed for me, the story of the Red Sea came back to me. I felt a gentle breeze blowing in my face. Me being me, I opened one eye to see if she was blowing in my face, but she had her head facing to my right. The wind got stronger and stronger, I could hardly stand, then a voice clearly said 'I am opening your Red Sea'. That was all I needed, I knew that God was working a miracle on our behalf, He was making a way where there seemed to be no way. Before the meeting had started someone slipped an envelope into my hand. I placed it into my pocket, and as I was leaving the meeting someone else gave me some money. When I got home we counted the money and God had given us £300.

Now there is a lesson for us all here, if you are feeling down, don't stay away from the meeting, God may have just the spiritual tonic you are in need of.

Wanting to have everything in order before going to Cyprus, we wrote to their embassy in London for any information they could give us concerning residency. They sent us a number of papers which were completely out of date. I phoned them and they were aware of this, but they had run out of up-to-date copies. They promised to send us a copy of the new papers, which they did by return of post. We received them, only to find that they too were out of date. The rules had changed a few months earlier. I phoned again only to be told they hadn't heard of any changes and maybe I should write to Cyprus.

I wrote to Cyprus and waited, after three months I wrote again thinking maybe they hadn't received our first letter. Another three months passed and we eventually received a reply to our first letter. It just said that we must first go on a tourist visa for three months, then apply for an extension. If we met all the necessary requirements an extension would be granted. We were still no further forward, no one would tell us what the 'necessary requirements' were.

Our minds were full of questions again. What if we give up everything here and then find after three months that we do not have the 'necessary requirements'? We had been told (incorrectly) that we could not rent a house until we had our extension visa. Where would we live for the first three months? I prayed, 'Lord please tell me, are we going to get an extension to our visa?'

Again during another of Marcel's sermons I was having a chat to the Lord (please note I did sometimes listen to his sermons, but at this time I had things weighing heavily on my mind). My bible just fell open in my lap to Acts chapter 18 and I only saw the first line of verse 11 'And he continued there a year . . .'

I wanted to shout 'Praise the Lord!' at the top of my voice. I knew in my heart that God had all these little details under control.

But where would we live for the first three months?

Chapter 17

The Move Is On

I woke up one Saturday morning with a tremendous burden for a lady I knew. I prayed and prayed and the burden just didn't lift at all. I shared it with Marcel and he suggested we went and visited her. So after lunch we went to see her. When we arrived she was looking great and as we sat down and she made us coffee, I'm thinking, 'Jen you've got it all wrong, she's fine, there's nothing wrong with her at all.' I didn't ask Marcel what he was thinking!

The conversation very soon got around to Cyprus. 'Are you sure that that is where God wants you?' she asked. 'Yes, we are very sure,' we replied.

'Then go,' she said. We then told her about having to find somewhere to live for the first three months and told her we were toying with the idea of going on a three-month package tour and finding somewhere to rent when we got our extension. 'Then go and book it' she said. If only she knew we still didn't have anything like the money we needed to go, let alone book a three-month package tour. We couldn't tell her we didn't have the money since we have only ever told the Lord of our needs.

'If you are really sure' she insisted, 'Go and book the package tour.' We must have looked a bit dumbfounded, for she added, 'And I'll pay.' She then hurried us out to get to the travel agent before it closed. I can't really explain how I felt, I was so happy I wanted to cry! I found myself praying, 'God, this is the sort of thing that I have read of in books, the sort of thing that always happens to some one else, but it is happening to us!'

When we got to the travel agent he had just one vacancy for a three-month booking. We knew in our hearts that we would be moving to Cyprus before the end of the year 1997 and the only date available was 28th December 1997.

It was booked, paid for and we were definitely going to Cyprus on that date. Now we had to think about getting rid of our furniture and possessions. Although we were in a furnished house we had still managed to collect quite a lot of things in seven years.

We were sharing with a friend how God had provided for us to book this package tour and we were definitely moving on the 28th December. He was delighted and praised the Lord with us. 'Jen, will you be selling your furniture?' he asked. 'Yes, the things that belong to us,' I answered. 'Well, can I buy your cleaner and the bedroom suite, and the television and the video. Oh and Marcel's desk and some of his bookcases?' 'God, this is great,' I thought, 'we haven't even advertized and already we are selling things.' God just seemed to have everything worked out for us.

In fact God had even provided a place where we can stay if ever we return to England. We are so blessed with the wonderful friends God has allowed us to have. Francis and Gwen are two of these special friends.

They used to live in Wilton and wanted to move closer to their church in Salisbury, so they put their house on the market. Then their time of testing began. Each time they found what they felt was the ideal place something would happen and the sale would fall through. We kept trying to encourage them by telling them that it had only fallen through because God had a better place. It was easy for us, we were not the ones going through all the stress and disappointments. Then when they found the place that God wanted them to have, everything just fell into place so quickly. They wanted a bungalow with a small garden. This bungalow was exactly what they were looking for and it had two dormer rooms built into the roof. These they decided would be a place for us to come to whenever we came home. One was made into a bedroom and one into a lounge. One of the large built-in cupboards was made into a toilet with a handbasin and the other a place where we could store anything we didn't want to get rid of. God was truly blessing them and working everything out to the finest detail for us.

Two weeks before Christmas God gave me a verse in 1 Peter 4 verse 12. 'Beloved think it not strange concerning the fiery trial which is to try you . . .' Something bad always happens when God gives me this verse and it did. A few days before Christmas at 1.40 a.m. our phone rang, Dad had been rushed to hospital and was having severe heart attacks. He was very ill and 87 years old. In my heart I knew it was God's will for us to go to Cyprus. I was having a big battle inside, but at the same time I had a peace. Although Dad's condition was very serious I knew we must go to Cyprus as planned.

Each day we went to the hospital to visit him, praying that God would work out His perfect will for us and Dad.

The day before we were due to leave England Dad's condition began to improve. In fact when we went in to say goodbye to him on the way to the airport, he was sitting out of bed and having a joke with another patient and they were both laughing very loudly. I knew we were doing the right thing.

Whilst we were packing we soon realized our luggage was very much overweight. I phoned the travel agent to see if we would be allowed to pay for excess luggage. I was told a very definite no. This was a charter flight and they had to be very strict about the amount of luggage anyone could take.

We were only taking two cases and two pieces of hand luggage, but we had packed rather more than one would normally get into the cases! So we decided we would just have to trust the Lord to get us through. Also as we were packing I found a ball of string and for some unknown reason I put it into my coat pocket.

Our friends Peg and Chris drove us to the airport and there was a lot of praying going on in both the front and back of the car. No, Chris wasn't driving badly, but we were all concerned about the luggage getting through.

When we got to the check-in desk the lady said 'Do you realise your luggage is overweight?' 'Yes,' I said, and explained that we were going to Cyprus to live and needed everything we had packed. 'I will have to charge you for the excess baggage' she said. I was quite prepared to pay, but she decided to only charge us half the cost. 'Thank you Lord,' we whispered to each other. After checking in and saying our good-byes we began to walk toward the departure lounge and the zip of Marcel's holdall broke, and guess who had a ball of string in her coat pocket! God knew that we would need it.

As we awaited the departure of the plane the fog got so thick that we could hardly see the buildings outside of the lounge window. All the incoming flights were late and many of the outgoing ones were cancelled. Our flight was two hours late and it was the last flight out of the airport that day. I felt so sorry for all the holiday makers with young children who had to spend the night at the airport but I was very thankful that we were able to go.

We watched fog-bound England disappear and four and a half hours later we were experiencing a very bumpy landing as we landed at Larnaca airport in the middle of a thunderstorm. The lashing rain stopped long enough for us to get into the airport and on to the coach which would take us to Ayia Napa. It then poured with rain until we reached our destination, stopping long enough for us to get our luggage into the apartment.

We arrived very tired but just so happy that at last the vision we had received thirty-one years earlier was now coming into being.

Chapter 18

Our Oasis Of Peace

We were very blessed with the holiday apartment in which we were to spend our first three months. It was in a very quiet block, with beautiful gardens and we had super neighbours who were also staying long term. In addition, we had the sun on our balcony all day.

On a previous visit we had met and made friends with some local people. They were very helpful and helped us in many ways to settle in. One particular lady, Elle, helped us to find a place to rent. She drove us to see many places. We were looking for a three-bedroomed furnished house, in a quiet location. Some of the houses were beautiful and in good locations, but they were all two-bedroomed.

Then one day she phoned, 'I think I may have found what you are looking for,' she said. 'It's a three-bedroomed, furnished house in Dherynia overlooking Famagusta Bay. Would you like to see it?'

Within a very short time we were on our way to see our first three-bedroomed house. The landlady only spoke Greek so it was good that Elle was with us. The house turned out to be an upstairs apartment and it was enormous, absolutely ideal for what we wanted. The moment we walked in the door we both knew that this was the place. The lounge had two sets of French windows leading out onto two balconies. The views were breathtaking. We could see the bay of Famagusta and the mountains in the background. There was a large open area which is the Green line of the border.

The kitchen was also very big and had lots of units with cupboards and drawers. This too had two sets of French windows leading onto balconies, one of the balconies was very large and the view overlooked Dherynia with the mountains in the background. It also had a brand new gas stove and a fridge freezer.

There were three bedrooms, all with fitted wardrobe units containing lots of cupboard space. In addition there was a utility room with built in sink unit, a bathroom/toilet with a shower and bath and second toilet with wash hand basin. The whole place was very clean and all the furniture was in very good condition. Our search was over. This was to be 'The Oasis of Peace' we had dreamed of for so long.

Some people have questioned why we didn't look for a bigger place, but we wanted a home of prayer, not an institution. We wanted people to be able to come and be part of our family. Those who have come so far have all been very glad of the peace and quiet and the individual attention we have been able to give them.

We actually moved in on the 1st March. Again Elle and her husband Andreas helped us in so many ways. We truly thank the Lord for them and for many others who so kindly gave us gifts to equip the home.

Our first visitors were due and we needed double sheets for their bed. So I went to a local shop that sold bedding and to my utter amazement they had sold out of double sheets. I went home thinking I would have to go into Paralimni the next day to buy some. But God had other plans. I had only been home a short time when the doorbell rang, it was a friend with a black plastic bag in his hand. 'My wife sent these for you,' he said and he left. I opened the bag, and there on the top were three double sheets. 'Thank you Lord,' I thought, 'before I called, you were there with the answer.'

Now we had the home, we needed to make it known to the workers in Israel that the home was available for them. We felt we really needed to visit Israel. So we prayed that if this was the Lord's perfect timing for us to go, then would He please release the necessary finance. 'Lord,' we prayed, 'please sell some more cows.'

The very next day we received two cheques from England for £5 each. I was sitting on the balcony thanking the Lord for these two gifts and it was just as if I heard an audible voice saying, 'Believe for more,' so I continued praying believing the Lord for all the money we needed for this trip to Israel.

Later that day someone placed an envelope into my hand and it contained several hundred pounds. We were so excited, for now we knew that this was the right time to go. In the next few days we received other gifts of money. We felt we should visit three different centres, and once again the dates we wanted were available in each centre.

Marcel had visited Israel before, but for me it was a totally new experience. I must admit I was very excited and a little bit apprehensive. So I prayed and asked the Lord to assure me of His protection, and He showed me a vision of Marcel and I with two very large angels which must have stood at least nine feet tall. They had their wings wrapped totally around us. I felt an instant sense of peace and knew that God had sent His angels to protect us.

The trip was wonderful, we met so many people all with a genuine love for the Jewish people. They came from so many countries with completely different backgrounds, yet they all had one common goal, to minister to the peoples of Israel. We learned more of the work amongst the Jewish people, the needs of the societies and workers. We came back armed with plenty of fuel for prayer.

The day we were due to return home to Cyprus I had put the alarm clock on to wake us up at the unearthly hour of 3 a.m. as the taxi was due to arrive at 4 a.m.

When I awoke I was having a dream that Marcel was having a diabetic hypo. I put the light on, looked at him and I knew he was definitely in a coma. I did all the usual things, but he didn't come out of it in the normal way. Time was going on, so I washed and dressed him and somehow got him down the stairs. He was far from well. I was dreading the thought of getting Marcel and our luggage up the stairs when we arrived home.

I was very relieved when we were actually in the air on our way home. That was until we got to Larnaca airport and found that all of our luggage had gone astray. I was so tired I could have burst into tears. After watching three plane-loads of luggage go around on the same conveyor belt, and keeping one eye on Marcel who was sitting down because he felt so ill, I was beginning to feel quite unwell myself.

It was then necessary to join another long queue of people who were all waiting to fill in claims forms because their luggage had either gone astray or items had been stolen. When it came to my turn the clerk said, 'What are you worried about, half of these people aren't even insured?'

'Yes,' I thought, 'but most of these people can walk into any shop and buy clothes off the peg, I can't.'

We were eventually sitting in a taxi on the last lap of our journey, Marcel was doing his best to cheer me up. I was so tired and worried, first about Marcel and now the lost luggage. Well, we did manage to get home without any further problems and it was only as we were climbing the stairs to our apartment that I realised I didn't have to carry the luggage up those stairs. Was this an answer to prayer? Two days later our luggage was delivered to our door safe and sound. The delivery man carried it up the stairs!

Chapter 19

Our Nightmare Begins

Once more back in Cyprus, Marcel's health continued to be a problem. So I suggested we went across to the hospital to see a doctor. After more than a little persuading Marcel agreed, only to be told his sugar was OK but his blood pressurc was up a bit. He should take some tablets and go every day to have his blood pressure checked. This he did for about ten days, but he was still very unwell.

We decided to go to the private clinic and just ask the doctors' advice and get something to help Marcel sleep. (He had hardly slept in two weeks.) After blood tests, an ultrasound and a bill for £90 we were no closer to finding out what was wrong. Then Marcel's condition became much worse, so I phoned the doctor and told him how poorly Marcel was, and could he please give him something to help him sleep. He said 'Of course. Bring Mr Desmet down now and I will give him something.'

We walked the fifteen minute walk to the clinic, by which time Marcel was ashen grey and feeling awful. The doctor called us in and began telling me off for doubting his diagnosis. As far as he was concerned, the only thing wrong with Marcel was that his sugar was out of control. I told him he had never taken so long to get over a hypo and I was sure something else was wrong. 'What do you mean?' he asked. I began telling him of the things that were happening to Marcel and he began to take notice. To cut a long conversation short, Marcel was asked to return to the clinic to see the neurologist in the afternoon.

He was then admitted to the clinic and a scan arranged for the following Monday. I returned home to get his clothes and insulin. I had only just got inside the door when the phone rang requesting that

I return to the clinic. It was necessary to take Marcel to Nicosia for an MRI scan immediately and the ambulance was waiting for me.

This was the start of a weekend I will never forget. I prayed all the way to Nicosia, 'God what is happening? We have waited over thirty years for this vision to come into being, in a few days time our first visitor is due to arrive from Israel and Marcel is so ill.'

For the next five hours Marcel was having tests. The doctor called me in and told me; 'Your husband has a bleeding brain tumour, but don't worry there's no cancer'. 'Will he be alright?' I asked. 'We don't know yet, we need to do more tests,' was the reply.

I eventually arrived home around 11.30 p.m. I was so scared, not of being in the apartment on my own, but for the future. I hadn't told anybody at this point, but two days earlier I had had a dream. In the dream first of all I saw my Dad in a coffin, (he had died three months earlier) then as I looked a second time it wasn't Dad but it was Marcel. A voice said, 'If Marcel died would you be willing to carry on the work here?' 'I don't know if I could,' I replied. 'I guess I would be willing to try with your help.'

Was Marcel going to die? I begged the Lord to heal him. The next morning I went back to the clinic and the doctor called me into his office again. This time he wanted to know who was going to pay for Marcel's treatment. We didn't have any medical insurance because the insurance companies aren't interested in insuring diabetics.

'What exactly is wrong with Marcel?' I asked. 'He's got a brain tumour and it's bleeding,' he replied.

'What treatment will he need?'

'We don't know yet, he needs more tests.'

Later that day I was called into the office again, this time to be told it wasn't a brain tumour but a tumour blocking the main artery to the brain. Marcel would need immediate brain surgery. We would have to go to England as they couldn't operate here, but he wouldn't be able to fly. There was one more test they must do, an angiogram, so I would need to be at the clinic at 6.15 in the morning to go to Nicosia by ambulance again.

I tried desperately to keep up a brave appearance when I was with

Marcel, but the moment I got back to our apartment I just couldn't stop crying. I phoned several people in England asking them to pray and my phone was going non-stop. I really appreciated every call, but I felt so lonely and scared. I really felt as if I was cracking up. 'God I can't cope,' I cried.

I felt I had to talk to somebody so I phoned a friend in England. I told her I felt as if I was cracking up, I just couldn't cope. I told her about the visit we were going to make to Nicosia the next morning. Looking back, I don't know what she thought of me, but being the friend she is, she was able to say just the things I needed to hear. I felt much calmer after our conversation.

The next morning at 4 a.m. English time this very special friend phoned me to check that I was alright and to let me know that she was praying for us as we travelled up to Nicosia. She always said the right things and encouraged me so much.

Our trip to Nicosia was quite frightening in many ways. The building we went to was like a rabbit warren, with endless corridors leading off into more corridors. The ceilings were very low and the whole place very claustrophobic. Everyone seemed to be shouting to each other in Greek and of course all the signs were in Greek. I remember thinking that if Marcel had to stay in this hospital I would never find my way in or out.

When Marcel was having his angiogram the builders were knocking a wall down in the corridor outside the room he was in, and wheeling barrelloads of dusty rubble through the crowded corridors. I was sitting in a corridor where people were going behind a small screen to have x-rays. It was an experience neither of us would like to go through again.

When we got back to the clinic we were told that it wasn't a tumour he had but a brain haemorrhage. I was relieved but also very angry that we had been put through all that stress, and that the people who were praying were getting so many different messages that they must have been totally confused.

It was now Monday night and I had just a couple of days to prepare for our first guest from Israel. Some folk suggested it would be better if I asked her not to come, but I knew this was the work that God called us here to do and I must do it.

I needed to do shopping, prepare the room, visit Marcel and try to get some rest, I was very tired and still cried a lot. I felt unable to eat but knew I must force myself to eat something. I hadn't eaten properly for about four days. 'Please God' I prayed, 'Send an angel to comfort me.'

The phone rang, it was Shirley from Kingsomborne in England. I greeted her with the words 'Shirley did you know you are an angel?' I did explain afterwards why I had said this. She is so caring and I could feel real love and concern as we talked. Being so far away from my friends made me rely on the Lord. It was very difficult but, praise God, He brought me through.

The following day the doctor called me into his office again saying that the bill for the past four days was already over £1,000 and I must pay it.

We had been told that Marcel would have to stay in the hospital for the next fourteen days having complete bed rest, then he would gradually be allowed to get mobile again. It was costing £50 a day without any medicines or treatment. I must admit I began to see the greatness of the bills and lose sight of the greatness of God's ability to meet those bills.

There was absolutely nothing I could do other than commit the bills into God's hands. I kept reminding Him that He had promised to supply all of our needs but there were times when my faith wavered.

I had a phone call from someone in England and he asked how much it had cost for the scan, I said, '£340'. He replied, 'Praise the Lord, Sis,' and began laughing. I didn't really feel it was a matter to laugh at, but then he continued, 'I placed £340 into your bank account this morning.' At this point we were both praising the Lord. I must say that the total bills to date have been around £2,700 Cyprus pounds and praise God, every cent has been provided for.

Back to our first visitor from Israel. A friend took me to the airport very early in the morning to meet our guest. I hadn't seen her before, so I stood waving my hand-made placard with her name on. Whilst we were waiting my friend and I were trying to guess what she would look like. Would she be old, middle-aged, dark, fair, tall or thin? We didn't have much to go on, I had only spoken to her a couple of times on the phone, but we were soon to find out. A very tired-looking lady wearing a wonderful smile, beamed in our direction. It just had to be Joyce. It was, and we were soon on our way home for a much needed rest. I think she just fell into bed and slept for the rest of the day, getting up for dinner in the evening. She said it wasn't until she came out of Israel that she realised she was carrying such a heaviness spiritually. This soon left her and she was sure she was going home a much lighter person spiritually, but probably a heavier person physically! I did my best to feed her well.

We enjoyed our meals on the balcony and our games of Scrabble. The fellowship was just what we both needed. She also visited Marcel in hospital, who was very disappointed not to be at home with us. When she left, Joyce wrote in our visitor's book, 'This weary warrior and worn-out saint goes back to Jerusalem very much rested and refreshed in body, soul and spirit.'

When Joyce went home I said to Marcel that I was sure she looked ten years younger. The next day I had a phone call from her and she said that all the folk in the office wanted to know what had happened to her in Cyprus, she looked at least ten years younger! I am so thankful that we were able to play a little part in helping Joyce to regain her strength so that she was able to go back to Israel and continue the wonderful work God has called her to.

Others have also visited and we count it a great joy and privilege to be able to share this Oasis of Peace with them, and to minister into their lives.

At the time of writing, Marcel is very much better and we are trusting the Lord for a complete healing. Praise God, all of our medical needs have been met.

Chapter 20

Looking Ahead

Now, as Marcel and I look back, we can see just how important it was for us to have a definite vision from God before setting out on this venture.

The trials have been many and the way hard. In our darkest moments it would have been very easy to have returned to England and received the natural security of the National Health system.

We would have loved at times to have visited a lively church service, or just spent an evening sharing fellowship with friends. There have been times when we have longed for a shower of rain, a frosty morning or just a cold breeze. As we have laid in bed at night too hot to sleep, and battled to get rid of cockroaches and creepy crawlies, it would have been so easy to give up and go home. The shortage of water and the dust storms are just a couple of the negative but very real situations we have to cope with on a daily basis.

But Praise God, He has kept us and kept the vision before us. He has remained faithful even when our faith wavered. He has given us His peace even when our whole world seemed to be falling apart.

It is our joy and privilege to work with God as He fulfils His plans and purposes for our lives and this Oasis of Peace.